Spoken Word Poetry

Molly Thokwana

Pharos Books

ISBN: 978-93-91103-92-7
eISBN: 978-93-91103-14-9

Publisher: Pharos Books (P) Ltd.
Plot No.-55, Main Mother Dairy Road
Pandav Nagar, East Delhi-110092
Phone: +14049995474
WhatsApp: +14049995474
E-mail: sales@pharosbooks.in
Website: www.pharosbooks.in
Edition: 2021

Spoken Word Poetry
Molly Thokwana

Contents

Preface

So many pieces in me have been broken and mended but still I stand. I would grieve in pain and my utterances would refer to "Gone with the Wind". In my previous life I lived the words, which could only uplift the broken and searching for something yet I know not what it is.

But withheld by the pain I had, I could only resemble and go through them. An island is better, I was a loner in words who spoke little though uplifted by the freedom of writing. The Dawn could be named after me, for I lived in grief of lost words and a hope I only dreamt to see in the wilderness.

Even a lane of lonely words explained nothing and the void in me searched a gospel; I only saw in light and noticed the reason why I felt nature was against me. It's because I had the light for it to fight against me.

I call this book: the little melody, were I write and my thoughts creatively tell epic poems that I call Spoken Word Poetry. A part of me could not express but words could. Words against words and a reflection of conflicted thoughts in one phrase.

I wrote more basically about my past and how I was saved. Concluded in the basics that hindered my life and my gifts. More so, my poems are about life, God and trials. Combined are story telling poems, in different forms. Written in form, from the first till the last poem.

Acknowledgements

I thank God for I am, what I am because of Him.

I thank my family and friends for being supportive of this book to be published. And I acknowledge every buyer who has bought a copy and read this book.

About The Author

Molly Thokwana is a writer, from Africa, Botswana born on the 4th of July. She is the author of twenty-one published books and has been working on many upcoming books. She writes in genres of short stories, motivational, adventurous, Christian writing, poetry and articles. She has also been published in places such as South Africa, India, Hong Kong, France and Botswana.

She is a graduate from Abm University College and holds an advanced diploma in Business Skills, and holds other qualifications in the fields of accounting and archives and records in literature field.

She completed her education from Aerodrome Primary, Selepa Junior, Mater-Spei College, Business Technical College and then progressed to Abm University College. She also shares some of her writings at poetmollymolz.wordpress.com.

A creative writer who is also a vocalist, song writer with her music playing on online music channels. She has worked with various producers and artists. Her music can be found online as Poet molz and her writings under the name Molly Thokwana on Google.

Void

A beat in my heart taps a thousand times
To an empty feeling
A roll that even deep down to me
Turns nothing but broken promises
That even sunshine's
Cannot reflect the beauty of nature in me
I cradle in ways that made my mays
turn into miracle violets

Singing songs that trumpets could not tune to
The dances that made me turn heads
And I could feel a rhythm control, worship in me
I felt Grace turned my mind to beautiful begginings
Reflections that even blinded mirrors
Darkness was a name but never existed in my mind

The mere run down
that can make my heart ache
even in memories
Broken beyond repairs
But mended Glory repaired

Even void feeling explain nothing but lost words
Trials turned into sun downs
I could have been a daughter's royal fate,
but my eyes were too bright
For the day light's

My written words dipped
no sorrow in all I wrote
But I laced through feelings
I could not catch

But the beat in me
Raves in melodies a saviour hears
That a void word or feeling made me
A kings daughter
Royal from the most high

The Last Poem

I wrote to unreason a forge
That sounds silent to the words untold

In the waters deeper than the seas
I cradle in summers like the weigh one sees

Beaten many times I lost in scattered loss
But the rhythm in me
Sings songs louder than bass
That even weapons shoot less

Sounded in my inner self
The sounds I beat in me only bad
I wrote a song, a poem, a word
But my feeling explain nothing
Because my pages were blank

To this last pages
I tossed in tense stages
This cold winters come in ages
So we walk through different faces

To the last poem
That makes me have thoughts

Of all this sages
From my inner most rough pages
I wrote words that forged not
To be heard of what I say and said

Rave of March

Another week of March,
my heart pounds to the empty promises
That spring leafs left with
The saddest goodbyes that
even morning can't take back

Another Wednesday of March,
a day before the saddest sounds
that even a rave beat cant speed
or the blind can't see

The memories that even a day
before yesterday
would not lane to remember
Another day of March,
were I sign a lil memory
that won't be forgotten

The only feeling that sleeps to my joy,
is the sunset
Autumn has taken my days

to walk no more in the mays
Another day, a poem arises in me
Another day of March a sandstones
written across my heart,
that only light greater than what
I withheld can break, the wines
that shun away my greatness
will resemble in the tongues of lost hope

Another week of March, I still believe…
In whose my heart holds the dearest
I write letters which long to be saved
The ones that even the winds blow
and I feel nothing
Just another rave,
of March and my precious memories

Could It Be

The one that every word
Aggressively intenses through the worst

The sounds that raves my lanes and bates
I dub thee a sermon of searching gospels

The feeling of shallow spears
unseen by wicked ones
The folds, we were never amused to see

Walked in the wines
of miracles but wanted more
The ungrateful who pleases to wage and sin
That randomly declares for their own

To the people,
The pupil
And to the pupils
Could it be,
We are blind

Yet we could see
Could it be
We lost hope

Could it be we reason in ways
That we never found profound to do
Or sage in, what we never seemed to be
Or we caged, in what we never wanted to have

Could it be?
This could all be a dream
We don't wake up to
But we feel

Paint My Words

Paint my words
And let this little light reflect in me

So I sermon the beauty of creation
Bree in me the astray of my words

So I scar your plead in this poem
Tell if justice is taking what is imprinted
And breaking the bonds without truth

When souls have been lost
Let not our hearts grow founder

But be found
For truth...

Tongue twists
Saged in the metaphors of heist

It was never legit,
so the streets could reflect
And words deflect...

Paint my words in sunsets
So I colour rainbows
And rain will have drops of sunrays

Paint my words
In many words
So my slithered tongue
Would praise every statue

From all your words
Paint
My words…

Maybe Just Maybe

Maybe I should write,
Write more till my hands are numb

Recite a silence of joy
When I'm sipping the eagers
of pain and hurt

Maybe I should have stood there
Within myself
Before myself
To the silent screams

That a million thought words, could tell
Maybe I should have cried
Before there
When it rained

So my eyes could sweep
away the pains
That made my heart
feel heavy and broken

Maybe I should have told you..
I wrote this in my sleep
across a thousand words
Just thinking
What if,
maybe just maybe…

Memories

Burn those ashes,
In the troops of blank pages
Align the glimpse of these tenses

As thy lips
Tips in red of scarred across

Let this be memories
When eyes couldn't see

And thy,
only remembrance of you
Let this be love
when melodies tune and tone

And this heartbeat
Raves beamer than the soundless

And melody sounds like nature
But remember the blank pages
They have those memories
Because you left none

Yet so loved and filled with joy
Your revival came in storms
So you forget the well
That made your rivers,
make you sink

Propaganda

Our war is deeper than World War 2
Life and thirst we put upon

We rendered the nations
bare footed for truth
and dare in those who misled us in pits

Who are we
Are we the sails you boat with,
when you want not to sink?

Or are we the army of your war?
We tail when you bloom even in winter?

We age even in shadows on lost patrols
In false written hopes
that were never written in any history

Our minds have enslaved
us to false promises
That made our tag lines seem
like we have insane our ways

Are we
Your restorations
to the plugs that fell
Your engraved truth,
to save you from sin to win
Is it peace to love
the ones you want to love

So we love to be fooled
Is it peace to Is it love of economy
To fall for the traps
That's never seized
to love the lost

So we are given promises
And all the heart
warnings fall into chances

Is it love
To fill up your minds with war
Yet we fight armless
To your battles that you only foreign
In the peace you only sovereign

Troubled Voice

Trying so hard to pick up the broken pieces
I even end up feeling broken
Stay up all night trying to figure it out
Wishing I did wake up to it
and call it a dream

Day and night it's the same thing
Mays and days come and go
I could only hear my voice
Hear my voice in all of these

Even trumpets shake not my inner self
I feel like a trap was built in me
To set fire to the ones who do wrong
At times I feel fire blazes in me
Even my smiles fade when it's just cold

I scream, but I hear my-self only
And the world is quiet
That's just
I'm just

A poet
with a troubled voice
Sent to save the troubled
Soul saving
Are you troubled?

Let Me Be Your Poet

Let me be your poet of the night
I will sing songs like fun the musician
Make it real like it's a live show
Listen to your every motion
to write a new poem

Over and over again…

Let me be your poet of the night
I will scrub walls when I'm out of paper
Paint my words in colourful pictures
I will crawl my words, to you
in distance like the war artisans

Write words in abbreviations
To dance to the rhythm of your tango
Drip more ink on paper
so you see my creative writing

Droll so many hearts across this paper
for you to believe I'm creative

If you let me be your poet of the night
This would be an all night prayer session

If you
Let me be your poet of the night
I will scrub walls when out of sight
Paint my words in colourful pictures
I will crawl my words, to you in distance
Like the air crafters

If you,
Let me be your poet
Of all times

Saved

I'm all here writing song metaphors
Beast can't touch me
I'm bond with the Holy Spirit
I got my tongue twisting like hair curls
The poetry slang scrubbed
on walls is now recited

The freedom speeches
have been chaffed with human rights
The less times are no more less times
Racism feeds on human minds
like a drug that can only be cured by Jesus

The cracks on minds blows
Now produce smoke like dull canvas We need God in everything
like daily chores
To be saved

I got my times
Reading defleted

But I know broken mirrors
even had me, reflected
I pray your saving is now not sometimes
So you flow
with the moments of being purified

I got words on my mind
Telling me we move like the wind
But times never revealed to such to find
Words never sealed to speak this kind

Just to find my way
Over places I went just to stay
To be saved

Grace Came Upon Me

My ink drips to the silent words that
Slithered through my tongue
in the sense of peace

Broken mirrors held me uptight when
all I could see on was the scriptures
That made my pain go away
A thousand times to an empty feeling,
I roll to the sun ways

To a prayer only a broken man
who believes not could kneel for
A scar that dims in the nights even
when the lights are switched on

There's a song of abbreviations
and heart ache that doesn't sing
in me no more
I dried my tears when I said
A thousand words
to the poems I wrote

Free handed, my other name could
have been named freedom
to the poems they wrote
and never sang songs of them
they made them lullabies to me

I found nothing worth holding on to
Their words at times
made me feel like daylight,
nightmares had started

Lost

I smile but deep down inside of me
I bleed sorrows of pain and hate
that could not be told

My past feels like yesterday,
a shadow I only forget and run away from
when I'm sleeping and laughing
but it's just for the mean time
I'm trapped in voices that told me
I couldn't make it when I'm already at the top

Misled by the beauty of creation
that a deeper cut can never heal
Even being justified is just a mere conclusion
of how to learn to hate your past
and try not to be your yesterday
The reason why dues and clues
can never ambition
but keep concluding with a conclusion

I only rave in the beats
that sounds even move more mere
with the city lights just to shine
when deep inside of me it's a bit dark
The pictures I took, the love I gave,
the pain I caused, the words I said
all feel void
The deeper cut, the one that reflects my tears
but I breathe into it day and night,
sulk in memories
that elude my own thinking

I have lost the sermons that told me
I could lift up a mountain
with the tip of my finger,
I have lost the words that told me
that I could shine even when
the sun doesn't reflect on me,
I have lost the sounds that told me
that a chain broken could break
another person's chain

I feel nothing but God's presence
that no Man can change or be trusted

but just God
But I'm lost in all the things
that the world holds for me
Simply in all my smiles and words
they all see the bigger picture
that hides deeper cuts that not even blades
can compete with or even swords,
but only God heals them

Empty

I could feel a thousand times
of my precious melodies
Sent and given in the nightfall's
like rain drops

A drip that injects pain
when deep outer me
I feel nothing but something
more than pressure

Drained but let allied
to define in pleasure
Take me away to words
that never told me
about cruel beginning's

The sun heats on me
like days that mays hoped to come
The sun got me burning
But words had me turning

I held a pen in illusion of dreaming
I could fly up high
but my troubles would still
have me spinning
The sad goodbyes

Nothing beats anything
more than the truth
Words from the saviour

Burns away all your troubles
And all the burdens I carried
Seemed to now be empty

I Really Have No Clue

I really have no clue what love is,
who to love or why to love?

I define my flaws and the pain
and love as just a fantasy

Sulked in the past I only feel the breeze
and the feeling that love once was told
In sincere words and flowers when love hurts

I have been told love is blind
So I loved with no feeling and learned
to love, but the love I gave away was a memory
of whom I love and dipped my words to

Tears that bid my mind
and made me taste love
would make my world end seized
To make me understand that I walked
in a rhythm not only probe by deaf jams
that summoned slow to whelm my mind
Probed in a melody like a trumpet,

uttered words only distance
and a proverb would reverse
until I learned to love God first
In all I did and do

Open Letter

My finger tips
Carve nothing but words

Thus solemnly,
raise a part of me which is broken
To write and paint
imaginary words like canvas

Wall beaten laid dices
That only rolled to broken houses
And broken dreams

Mended by grace that
Man not know of
When God creates even memories
one can smile to when sleeping

A beat in me never told me
Rhythm created all the words
But feeling created all the words I wrote
And God is the creator of all

Because of the ways
I prayed and His says
I am Reborn….

Memorized Mind

Through my imagination
and the words I would write,
I would imagine you short

The sun would literally
never even block your view,
but mine I would dash on sun heat hash tags
and write about them all day

I would smile to the roses
and my heart would still feel drowned
when I imagine how short you are

I would literally walk across dashboards
and because you have no goals
you walk even through them

Times would pass
and love would be the other name,
of why people should blame
who they love not love itself

I would write poems at times
and you would even put coffee cups
to wipe away stains from tables
with sincerely my words and heartbeat
You would take it all away from me
My smiles, my words, my worth and my dreams…
You would think
I am the perfect match in your world,
by spiritual lack you would make more bars
on Sundays and make me ring bells on tells
I would literally be the lost and praise
who got fooled by love

My name will write only blue words
on Mondays after weekends,
and pray mcm's don't cross my mind
I would be called names because of imagining
that love is just another obsession a journal
would not write to

Days would go and our little moments
would be changed to who short listed you
I would daily write about God and you

would sincerely never know the wonders I feel
A part of me would be broken if I ever
loved, a short listed
who is short of words like you
through my mesmorised mind

Still Confession

A part of me it's broken,
but I still speak
It's like the universe,
never wrote about me yet I exist

A few scars made me
build a few blocks
up my life but everytime
I see trees
I can't be shaken

The wind blows before me,
I sip in silence that even a low voice
reflects in the midst of it
A reflection of me in broken mirrors,
wrote that love was a fantasy

I overdosed in it to hide my scars
in the prettiest memories
I write about even gone with the winds
could never blow in the same direction

A piece of me told me stories
that tales could not be misunderstood or told
A hole in me, was patched by Glory
and I held my hand so high and
It wasn't dark anymore
I smiled In the inner sides of me,
broken in failures that weren't mine
but I prayed for them, I prayed that my light
be shared in ways that even half's
could not be pronounced

A piece of me stolen by a still confession,
the one that even a poem
had to be written thirty times thirty
to be composed
and a freedom in me still felt empty

They called me a confessed confessor,
because I had my first breath taken away
by a mind that reflected the same as mine
but burnt more fire that I couldn't handle

Even my knee caps almost bent down
and I felt Glory had come

and my time to pay my dues was up
I laid my hand in the most unspoken words
that I uttered in my silence and everytime
I felt this words made me free

I still wrote a few more
to doubt my ways
and question myself

Could I be the ways that creation
had me but turned out to be
the saddest writer who found happiness
in every last word she wrote?
A breath in me got taken away
by songs and actions

I held my head up high hoping
the heavens would fall on me,
so I could stop confessing
and confuse the words

Even love hurts not this bad,
I trembled in my voice sounds
that cold winds would answer to

A thought I had but could not sing to,
I resembled the suns of sons even
in confusion to try and mislead and lead

But a silence in me healed wounds
that lies had broken
A sane I only imagine but cant tell,
its like I lost something yet its there
and I cant find it

A smile I feel yet it makes me weaker
I sign memories in words
you said and never made them
A fantasy I have never seen
yet I imagine, across a heartbeat

I cannot explain a dawn that confuses
my imagination if words can be true
or truth can be an illusion
I feel nothing, yet I love something,
trials could not be this long
It's a trial that ends in nightmares
and I pray about

Love Me Not

My heart wrote words that
even a faded mind could compose
in metaphors and verbs
Love was blind when blind dates
were blind folded and a letter could tell
a million words but no love
I swear even the truth could not resemble
Love not and made it Love me not
A song plays in me that makes me see
winds when they cant be seen and
I prefer love as an illusion that
makes love to be complicated

I wrote this poem blind folded in feelings
so I would love not and write the past
The sun burns away a piece of me
that was never written but I imagine it
Consoled in a memory that
I cant remember in a song that sings
in a silence of still minds

I was told my imagination could create
freedom with the thoughts I have,
so I made reality a verb that could
adjust to the questions that may make
a probability seem to be just an imagination
My reasons could not be withheld,
I questioned even the questions
and even made love question its own word
that love could not be love if loved
not or how to love

A thousand words I wrote and still I had
urge to ask how to uphold and I found nothing
I noticed in love it was a confliction between me
and my mind that questioning love
is like questioning why feelings exist
I breath love air, yet they said it painted
the world and made some suffer

Impartation the mysteries,
yet I could not tell and forged
beyond lies and heartbeats was just a thought
And I came to imagine, love does not hurt
The person you love is the problem

If Love Was A Song

If love was a song
I would tap to this feeling
rail to the rhythm of this way for healing
cross hearts in melodies
so my words could be sang

Dance in astray
and keep you in every word I pray
so my words could be a replay

If love was a song
words I write would be this long
sane and dipped in melodies I sang
every heartbeat would not be wrong

But if love was a song
I would sing about it write about it
talk about it
pray about it
and think about it .....

If only love
Would have been a song
It would be this poem long ❍

Reflections

I still see a part of me in broken mirrors
That cut me deep
Wounds I couldn't heal
but holes left with pitches

Voices I could hear
but times couldn't reveal
I wish to be a reflection
Let lit in words

That speak silence through eyes
a thousand times through pain
I wish to be a reflection
To be reborn
And make the born, be reborn

Her, To The She

She writes my heart to the deepest cores
that can't be dug out, this feel deep
The winds that only blew west,
when I came in from the east
Similes could make me sound
like I stammer in her presence

Suns turn to cloud nine
when she passes by
A beat of me sang rhythms
that even the heat could not produce
I smile in the ways of low sounds
I hum to, in presence of this she
Warm folds unfold even in winters

The songs I produce that I never wrote
The summers that slow heats
that cant reflect on me
Her to the She Is my loving mother…
The dear mother to me….

A silence echoes her presence
I still see a part of me In broken mirrors

That make me grieve her presence

That lays with angels
She was a piece art could not define
That love unfolds to happiness
She is, she was a loving mother

That Cut Me Deep

Before me stays panthers
I can never touch
Nor recall to my lone
that tears me down
Broken in hunger of pieces
that bring my world down
The letters I wrote in my silence
Could not be let lit

A smile that faded in my repentance
A rain came and washed away my sins
If I was tall enough
I could reach out to the heavens for blessings
A voice from the truth,
I read revolts all of it
As winds that passes with the seasons....

A broken hole wrecked in silence
and spoken in cast Black lipstick
Dark as the ways that
even tunnels could not light to

Prayer in the unspoken words
A moment that even memories
can't write to
A part of me makes me imagine
that if lies and heart beat could transform
A full part could overwhelm
the joy that smiles over me

At times a part of me seems
to overwhelm me in the words
I never wrote
That trouble, could not be broken
down and I wrote illiterate

Stitches

Stiches in my heart burnt me
a thousand times
To the empty promises that left
my miracles looking void stars

Couldn't reflect my future so well
So I let Glory take charge of the ways,
that let me loose in the mornings
Indecent minds we ralph in our hearts,

A silent little prayer
that makes us believe
That hope is existence
The pounds and the pains deep,
we sink in faith

That we can't even make
it through the indecisive...

Tears To My Song

The songs I write are endless,
the melody has no chorus no happiness
my joy underneath

All my troubles and the bitter notes
to my songs are dull and full of anger
Faraway places in a sacred place were no
harm can be bound

The heartbeat and mood to my songs
have a low sad sound
Tears droll away my sorrows
when I sing this song to free myself

I am Not Sure

I'm not sure if I am a poet,
but I spend days in dripping silence
of my pen only heard by me

The eager and anger and feeling
that abuses my soul of innocence

I am not sure if I am a poet,
but I keep drilling my nails to the finish
my poems reciting words only poets speak

But still, I am not sure I am a poet
because I write few words
to be heard and inspire
Yet my utterance shivers
not even in the cold,
I am not sure if I am a poet...

Thoughts

I lied for you
Stole words
from innocent souls for you,

Walked in your thoughts
When your silence,
hallowed thoughts in me

That could not be ranked and rated
I begged for you
Even the poor hated my ways
But I walked in innocence and prays

Still forgiveness rooted my ways
For my direction was poured with greatness
only deflected, I sang for you

Even sweet melodies
could not compose words
And sometimes my voice sounded
worse than your troubles

I lied to you
In the midst a half of me felt
forgotten and lost in me
So we did forget
This are just thoughts
I am having on a Saturday morning

Self Portrait

I rhyme in the cores
That melt my heart
as bolt as the hearts I sketch
Bruised in mankind

I sing a silence sonnet
In the suns of the sons
I couldn't bring
Written my name
an anthology could not uphold

Smattered in my lips
To the heavens
I only had sips of love heating
That love songs found me seating

And I danced to mercy
and He only made me know it all
I let this pray pound in me
But a piece of me told me
Broken or repaired

I still had a self portrait
That man do not write of
But life is not a fantasy
of what heat could not bring forth

Loose

I wrote a letter to my pains
That my tears dried,
with the winds

The sun couldn't shine on me
My skin reflected light even
heavens couldn't hold

A song I sang in the silent waves
I only waved in the inner
ways that sounded numb

My heart beat only
saved the memories
A part of me never said
Even solo rythms
skipped a half of me
I lost my ways
when times could not tell
I could upsurge the pages of weigh
And a part of me
Never waved to the pains

Drowned

A part of me writes sincerely
To words I never thought
exalts a part of me
Painted in numbers
that count nothing
A silent melody I listen to
But I came with a broken mind
that told me about weakness
Dark skin girl Worn in a dark blue dress
Written above was a dark black scribble
The one that writes nothing
But wakes me up from this dream
And feels all my troubles are drowning

Untold

I smiled, through my struggles
and my heart breaks
I couldn't breath on, still smiled
To the light that didn't seem bright
enough and I wore a mask

I couldn't feel I still smiled
When pain hit me down and hate
couldn't resist me, I still smiled
My head over it all, I still smiled

A piece of me broke memories
I reached out to, I still smiled
left in memories that sang solo songs
with no beats and I felt like
I held the acoustic in me, I still smiled

The purge that lit my life up
and I drew side papers on the edge
of my heart beat, I still smiled

A part of me broke down
a million words
I couldn't recite
Left in the lone
I felt the urge to still smile

Loved Wrong

Look into my joy
And see every piece of me
that you broke that went away
I forgot all about the pieces
I couldn't hold up
That even bright memories
made them look black

A vanity of women
Shaded in silence
That only the broken ones
could hear

A letter was written to you
But cheap things never touched your soul
I could hear praises a thousand miles
Like yesterday never came

Smokes that made me see
Could not even bring me down

Look at me now
And tell me
If you see a broken soul
Or a soul
that can break you now

Remember Me ?

Remember me when I used to care
And you treated me like a broken mirror
Even side burns don't hurt this bad

I felt the sun reflected not in me
Now im cold as the untold seasons
And a sad story I tell in the night falls

The ones that even stones can't carve to
A smile that prunes my heart
into sad little memories
Diamonds turn black to my resistance

Its like days could never be reversed
A part of my heart beat in words I wrote
A three times six that turns into ten
Impossibilities caused by nature
and captivated by beauty that
could not be accepted

Remember me,
I even crawled on my knees

that pierced my heart
To believing in faith….
That all this
Is one unforgeateble memory

Ript

I found myself sniffing in words
that made my freedom less
of the words I wrote,
The insanity that left me
breathing low selfless
such words, that could never be told
Even if my hands
curved wood in the places
I could not imagine

They all called it search of the light
Where even words less portray visions
that ecstasy could not fill
The void that left the foul
to feel no breeze

Even if a ballad
was two words songs
could not be sang but loosened
I find it left in marks of no words
that visions could not be seen but felt

The Voices....

Everytime I rolled my hands in works,
a word in me made me sink in sermons
I wrote and thought of
The part were freedom is enslaved
by direction, had my turns named
after the pain I patched in my own

freedom of mind
I could slither the least words
I came across but a melody
that dimmed all my joy made my pages
turn blank even if I wrote

A thought that made me dream in daylight
and believe light could be passed on
I held a sword that left loose
in appoints of Christ presence
A beat in me sang solo songs
when all the chains I had broken loose

I left a day when my melodies had nothing
but tramped troubles of forgotten ways

My say's and the one thing that saved my soul
in all the prays was God
I scribbled till my words could
not be understood and some said
I spoke in tongues, but my mind twisted
only the great of the greatest
and I vowed a word to be saved

A pure lil light had me seeing words
that I made a turn to
and never curved even in scribbles
My hands found nothing
but void to the words I wrote

I called freely with a piece of me broken
to a mend that lifted me high
And all of it, fell apart
when I prayed and wrote

But they couldn't understand,
because only who made me,
could break just a piece of me
but not harm me
Broken but built to live
beyond measures

Imagine

I'm going to marvel
and let my mind unravel

Imagine I'm in heaven
and let allied my pains
and trials walk away from me

Reveal the child's and child's act
in me so i enter the heavens kingdom
Through words in a land of paper and pen

Saddle in paddles on illusions of my poetry
Through the water in canoes with a paddle
and imagine
What if I was a Moses

Imagine I could sip God's love
and sign wonders in silence
Through the air in a plane
with the flight admiral and imagine
I'm a bird and I could fly
Look down on nature's most beautiful,

battles and say I'm higher
than all my trials

Saddle in the sands of God,
given hands and pray
Relate to the sad words
and believe I'm an overcomer
I'm going to imagine I'm more,
than all my trails and defeat them
So I just imagine all this..

Just If, If

If my fate dies,
and all I search for
is burnt wood
Then the sermons
that woke me when I was blind
and my heart pounded a thousand times
of burn, will I not purify the souls
of the righteous but
write away the troubles
That not even man can wage

Let the eyes that even open even
when the light doesn't shine
and I can still see
A memory that reflects
on a thousand mirrors
with a scar and a song
with the saddest goodbyes

That a guitar can tune to
If I wake up and all I breath is void,
then let justice prevail....
Just an if, if

Earth

I drafted my heart in a sketch
metaphors that couldn't reflect
even as bright as the stars
pierced by pain

I felt bare by my emotions
wrote a symphony to sing
love live love
a silent melody echoed

as I browsed through the nights
I forsake the dark in the
lightens of the moons nights
breathing in the breeze

the little light sound
left me in greed of poems
scribbling in the sand
A gaze that had made me hope
was Heaven on Earth

Dear Rhythm Beats

My heart beats an extra mile
to the beats that make my melody
turn into sunshine's
The rave that makes me move

even when the dance tunes
in me are loose
I find myself grasping in
low sounds of betrayed echoes
To the names that made me

Lose control I wrote a thousand times
of empty letters feeling need to say
nothing but describe my empty feeling

Laid in the moments
I pounded an extra more times
I could hold my world
And the beats would be
my sun and shine on me